D0835356

Irish
Home
Essentials

First published 2016 by The O'Brien Press Ltd.,
12 Terenure Road East, Rathgar, Dublin 6, D06 HD27, Ireland.
Tel: +353 1 4923333; Fax: +353 1 4922777
E-mail: books@obrien.ie
Website: www.obrien.ie
ISBN: 978-184717-881-7

9 8 7 6 5 4 3 2 1
19 18 17 16

Layout and design: The O'Brien Press Ltd.

Printed and bound Printed and bound in the Czech Republic by
Finidr Ltd.

The paper in this book is produced using pulp from
managed forests.

Irish
Home
Essentials

Seamus Ó Conaill

THE O'BRIEN PRESS
DUBLIN

~POSH~ ~BAG~

'Keep that nice now. It'll be handy for bringing presents to the neighbours.'

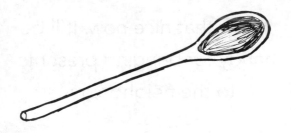

'Hand out! I said, hand out!'

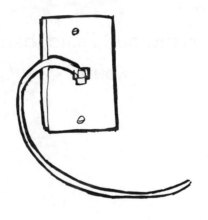

Shshshshsh ... crrrr ... shhh
... brrr-grrr ... shhhhh ...
'You off the internet yet?
Nana will be ringing.'

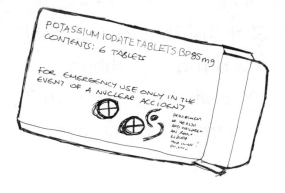

'For emergency use in the event of a nuclear accident.' (Exp 2005)

unopened

'Sweet Jesus, where's the highlighter?'

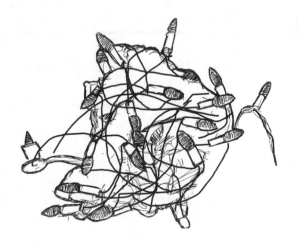

'No, you turn, yes, back, and twist, and lift that through there … now turn, and if you put your hand through there and I do this … no, that's caught now. You step back and catch that end there, and I'll put my fingers in that tangle and you turn your … no, no, no! Ah, here Feck it! Now you put your hand through there. No, you turn … yes, back, and twist, and lift that through there, now turn, and if you put your hand through there and I do this …'

'First place in the egg and spoon. Fair play, we'll keep that out for Nana.'

'I've got hives, I've got a sting, I've grazed my knee, I've got a paper cut, I've got a burn, I've got a spot. I've got a wart. I've a sore leg. I've a broken wrist. I've chest pains. My arm is tingling. Oh, help me, God, I'm dying ...'

'We'll hang on to it. You never know.'

*Soon to sit beside the
pressure cooker*

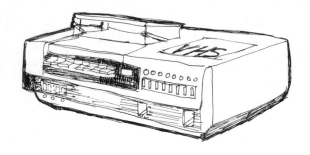

'Did you rewind it? You have to or we'll get a fine.'

'Will I deflate it?'
'No! I might use it yet ...
Look, I'll put a slipper there
so it won't be rolling round
the study.'

'Watch my walls!'

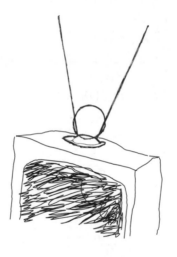

'No. To the left. If you stand there … but when you move … Now, literally just a touch. That's too far now! It's gone! Back! Back!'

Blesses self

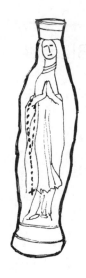

'A splash on the car and we won't be needing insurance.'

'Would she ever give them a wash? She's showing up the road.'

POT
POURRI

dust collector

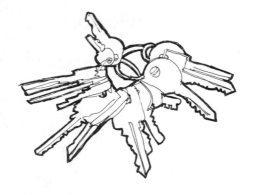

'No. It's the one on the other loop. No, that's for work. That's the garage. That's Granny's. That's the neighbours ...'
'... just give them to me!'

'Try that one. Not the one the dog chewed. The one with the sellotape holding in the batteries.'

'Keep that now. It'll be handy for buttons.'

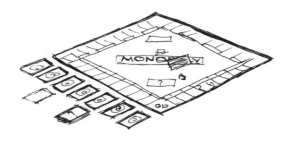

'You've been nicking money from the bank.'
'No, I haven't.'
'Then how'd you get that place on Shrewsbury Road?'

'Bit of butter and a few crisps. Heaven.'

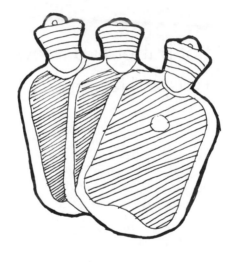

'Can't we just put on
the heating?'
'NO.'

TINSEL

'Mam! It's not the 80s!
Nobody puts that up
anymore!'
'That's their business.'

'We'll fill them back up with tea. Daddy won't even notice.'

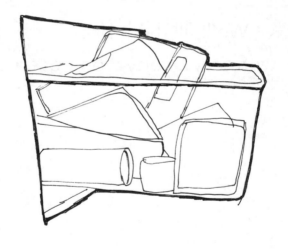

'Try that lid. No. Try that one. No. That one? No ... Do any of them match at all?'

Broken earphones, two cent coins, another
set of broken earphones, Sellotape where
no one can find the start, a Nokia 3310
phone charger, plug adapters for Spain, a
broken pen, dry highlighters, more broken
earphones, a tangle of leads, a hairbrush
with unknown hair in it, a clothes brush,
a soother, a snapped necklace, toys from
a Kinder Egg, a small Vaseline lip-balm
tin, a broken Dictaphone, old batteries, a
knob off an electronic device from the early
nineties, chopsticks from a local Chinese
takeaway, a Christmas tree bauble, a yo-yo,
a superglue tube stuck to the bottom of the
drawer ...

Bath towels, small hand towels, grey-ish towels to dry the floor, towels for the gym, tea towels ... and a bed for Mittens.

*Five members of family ...
sixteen toothbrushes*

looks at soap, pulls face, rinses tips of fingers, and wipes hands on trousers

'The tape's all chewed.
Have ye a pencil?'

'Oooonly a woman.
Ooooonly a woman ...'

'And you get this free with
your Ray-Bans.'
'Oh ... thanks ...'

'But how does it work?'
'God knows.'
'It'll be handy for washing
the dog, anyway.'

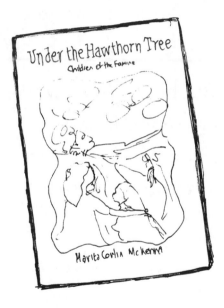

'Keep that good now, your brothers and sisters will be needing it after you.'

'There, now. That'll keep
them good for your
brothers.'

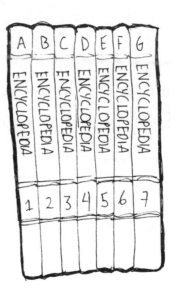

The Monarchs of England ...
George VI, 1820-1830
William VI, 1830-1837,
Victoria, 1837-Present Day

'Stop picking at the chips!'

84

'Daaad, why's that coming
in the post?'
'Ask Nana.'

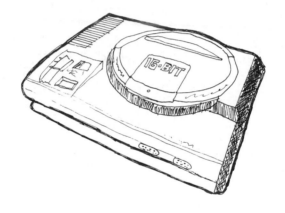

'SAY-GAAAAAA!'

National Irish Bank Statement August
2001, receipt for Apple computer
1988, receipt for 14" television
23 May 1990, lira from holiday to
Rome 1999, Quinnsworth receipt
26 September 1994, a few hair
grips (hairs attached), punts, Texas
Homecare receipt, Anko form 1988,
Windows 95 CD, birth certificates
as yellowed and fragile as the Turin
Shroud, two floppy discs ...

Eerily clean *tick*
White lace armrests *tick*
Strangely quiet *tick*
Faint damp smell *tick*
Freezing cold *tick*
Fake electric fire that's
never been turned on
tick

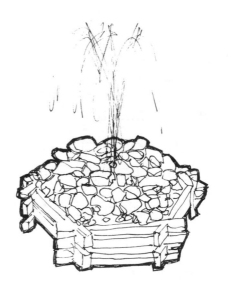

Because Diarmuid Gavin did a fabulous one on the telly last month.

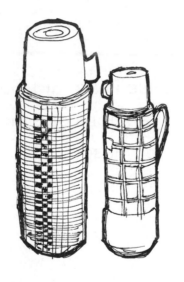

B.C.*

*Before Costa.

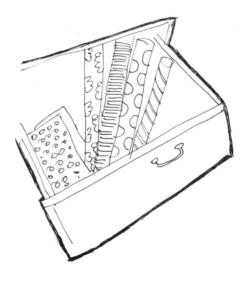

'Jesus, don't rip it! We can use that again.'

'Mam, I can't find the doll's adoption papers!'

'Why did we ever take it out of the box and enjoy it? We could've paid off the mortgage.'

MAGIC STEPS

'Just trust your Magic Shoes ...'

'So, all I want is that and that and that. Oh ... and that and that and that and that and that, and mayyyybe that ...'

'I won't be replacing the batteries. You hear me?'

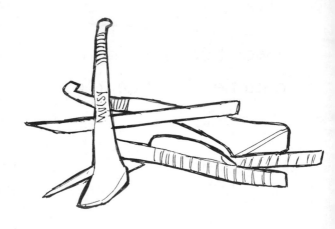

'Stop hitting your brother!'

To School Through The Fields

ALICE TAYLOR

'D'you remember ...'

'The pencil goes *where*?'

CYBERPETS

The number-one cause of pre-teen neuroses c.1997.

'They'll be grand. Sure, that's fifty quid saved on a prescription.'

118

'Weren't we supposed to
send that back?'

THE DEATHS

FITZGERALD, Geral.

HICKE

HOGAN

'Fantastic. I outlived that aul bastard, God rest his soul ...'

TDs, councillors, fast food, gutter-cleaning, Lidl, Woodies, Harvey Norman ...

still unsolved

1980s: Scattered around the house.
1990s: In a drawer and pulled out at parties.
2000s: Windowsill, back yard.

Wine bottles spreading out, slowly taking over the utility room
'Should we head to the bottle bank?'
'Next week, next week.'

'Can that go in the recycling or is it a book?'

One day in May ...

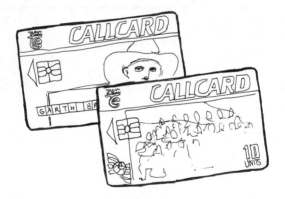

'I've only one credit left.
Call me back.'

'You can't give that away. That was a wedding present.'

'Why would you be paying
for glasses?'

'The head on me. Two months more and the braces would've been off.'

'Mam, do we have glue?'

'Mam, have we any Blu-Tack?'

'Mam, do we have tissue
paper?'

'Mam, do you have any string?'

'Mam, have we any greaseproof
paper?'

'Mam, where's the thumb
tacks?'

'Mam ... Mam ... MAM ... I need
a scissors ... MAAAAM ...'

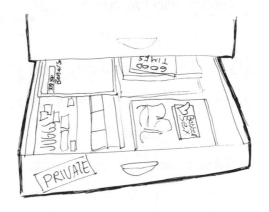

'Any johnnies?'
horrified pause
'You can't get pregnant the
first time anyway.'

'Can we get Frosties ... can
we? Please ... '
'No. I don't care what your
cousin Barry gets.'
'Pleeeeease ...'

'Double Velvet? Must be visitors coming.'

... and black.

'So, you'll be needing four fillings, a crown, two extractions and a root canal.'

'Sail away, sail away, sail away ... '

'Now hands that do dishes ...'

Get busy with the fizzy ...

So how Irish is your home?

You've fewer than 30 'essentials' in your home ...
Say a prayer to Saint Jude. Your house is a lost cause.

You've 30-40 'essentials' in your home ...
Better start hanging a few Sacred Hearts around the place.

You've 40-50 'essentials' in your home ...
Well done. Treat yourself to a cup of tea in the 'good room'.

You've over 50 'essentials' in your home ...
Bualadh bos, a chara! Your home is the pride of Ireland.